Circle of Stones

Reviews of CIRCLE OF STONES

A book of healing . . .

"This is a book about women helping women, about mentoring and bonding, and about the sacredness of women 'being there' for each other at all stages of life. [It] deals directly and gently with women's pain, depression, sorrow, and tears, re-consecrating them as valid. [It is a] book that touches women's souls and helps to heal."—*Pilgrimage*

A book for the heart . . .

"A gentle, wise little book that speaks to the heart —and hits home. A book to be given to mothers and sisters and girlfriends for birthdays and Christmas and no reason at all."—*The Sunday Oregonian*

A personal journey to the Feminine . . .

"Judith Duerk takes us on a personal yet universal journey to the essence of the Feminine. In an intimate and richly woven style, she weaves a tapestry that reaches far back in time, yet grounds us in the lives of women today and in the future. As the stories, dreams, and visions of women unfold, we are called to honor the Feminine in ourselves, in each other, and in the world."—Lucia Capacchione, Author of *The Power of Your Other Hand* and *The Creative Journal*

A 'gem' that makes a difference . . .

"*Circle of Stones* is one of those book gems that enters a person's life and makes a difference. Its impact is powerful. The one-page scenarios, which begin and end with 'How might your life have been different if . . .' are so moving, I found myself crying in response to them."—Owner of Stiles for Relaxation (Portland, OR)

A welcoming guide to inner wisdom . . .

"*Circle of Stones* draws us gently into a meditative experience of the lost feminine. Judith Duerk's discussion of depression and illness as gifts that force women to listen to their inner voice reminds me as a therapist to respect the nurturance and fertility in these processes. A welcoming, loving guide for women seeking to find a path to their own inner wisdom."
—Anne M. Berlin, Ph.D., Psychologist in Private Practice

A compelling call to personal discovery . . .

"A book of compelling integrity . . . the central axis around which this book evolves is that woman's spirit-self is found in solitude, in recognizing the validity and truth of her own feeling values, and that one's personhood is not found in safe conformity to outer values but in the darkness of personal discovery."—Christella Carbaugh, SLW, Coordinator of Spiritual Life, Sisters of the Living Word

A book of surprising truths . . .

"*Circle of Stones* flows easily, ceaselessly cushioning us with delightful and surprising truths. Judith's lovely book for women is a rewarding journey. Highly recommended."—*Spiritual Studies Center Booknews*

An invitation to the inward journey . . .

"*Circle of Stones* is more than a call to reflection . . . it is a beckoning to go forward, for each woman to make the journey to herself. It causes [us] to acknowledge [our] deep indebtedness to those women who are present to [us] on this journey, and challenges [us] to be open and present to others. An excellent book; recommended reading for all women."
—*Catholic Library World*

The best gift . . .

"If there were only one gift I could give to all of my women friends, this book would be it. It speaks powerfully to many emotions, issues, and lifeways common to women . . . and brings home the important reality of 'Woman's time' as different, slower, more in tune with natural cycles . . . a part of the deeper, more sacred center."—*Intuitive Explorations*

A voice for the lost Feminine . . .

"*Circle of Stones* speaks to the part of us that mourns silently for what has been lost to the world since patriarchy became the order of the day. It jogs our ancient memory, that deep part of us that somehow *knows* that there were ancient lands where the Feminine was revered. *Circle of Stones* is a book I devoured. Several of my friends say that this is one of the most important books of their lives."—*Chinaberry Catalog*

A book of empowering . . .

"I am recommending this book to all women. I started to pick out parts to quote to women and realized I could settle for nothing but the whole. It's a short book, but every page is accepting, healing, empowering."—Kay Bradway, Ph.D., Founding Member of the C. G. Jung Institute of San Francisco; Author of *Villa of Mysteries* and co-author of *Sandplay: Silent Workshop of the Psyche*

An essential book for women . . .

"*Circle of Stones* continues to serve as a threshold for thousands of women waking up to the essential questions of consciousness."—Christina Baldwin, Author of *Calling the Circle: The First and Future Culture* and Co-founder of Peer Spirit Circling

A touching, transformative read . . .

"I could not put *Circle of Stones* down. I wondered if this book itself is particularly magnetizing or if it came at the 'right' time. In picking it up a second time, I realized that the book speaks to me on many different levels and would, I'm certain, touch a chord in (almost) every reader at any time. I give this review in hopes that others will pick it up and find their lives becoming transformative, powerful, different." —*Booknotes* from the Center for Women and Religion

A meditative experience . . .

"I am recommending *Circle of Stones* to every woman who walks into the store. This marvelous book is the story of a woman's journey to herself. Duerk draws us gently into a meditative experience of the lost Feminine. She creates the female space for us to consider our present lives from the eyes of women's ancient culture and ritual. Read this book!"—Lucia's Garden Newsletter (Houston, TX)

CIRCLE OF STONES SERIES

BY JUDITH DUERK

CIRCLE OF STONES:
Woman's Journey To Herself

I SIT LISTENING TO THE WIND:
Woman's Encounter Within Herself

THE CIRCLE CONTINUES:
Women Respond to Circle of Stones

circle of stones

JUDITH DUERK

woman's journey to Herself

INNER OCEAN PUBLISHING

MAUI, HAWAII   SAN FRANCISCO, CALIFORNIA

Inner Ocean Publishing, Inc.
P.O. Box 1239
Makawao, Maui, HI 96768-1239

Originally published by Innisfree Press, Inc.

For information on promotions, bulk purchases, premiums,
or educational use, please contact: 866.731.2216 or
sales@innerocean.com.

Publisher Cataloging-in-Publication Data
Duerk, Judith.
Circle of stones : woman's journey to herself / by Judith Duerk. —
15th anniversary ed. — Makawao, HI : Inner Ocean, 2004.
p. ; cm.
(Circle of stones series ; v. 1)
ISBN: 1-880913-63-1
1. Women—Psychology. 2. Women—Identity. 3. Femininity.
4. Identity (Psychology) 5. Sex role. I. Title.
HQ1206 .D84 2004
155.6/33—dc22   0408

Acknowledgements

My thanks to the women who have allowed the use of their dreams and writings, and to the women of the original circle for whom this writing was begun.

My acknowledgment to Susan Stark and Elizabeth Gould-Leger for their skills and sensitivity in preparing early stages of this writing, and to Ruth Butler for her insights and assistance in later stages. My appreciation to Marcia Broucek of Innisfree Press for her kindness and warmth.

And my gratitude to my husband, John, and to my two sons, Adam and Joshua, for their steadfast encouragement. This writing from the feminine truly was "brought to expression on a platform carefully prepared by the supportive masculine."

to my sister and my brother
and to Faith

Contents

Preface

Circles of stones, haunting, healing, powerful . . . from the ancient circles, the Ring of Brogar in the Orkneys, the Rollright Stones, Stonehenge . . . to the dozens, perhaps hundreds of circles in Scandinavia and the northern isles . . .

Circles of smooth stones on a table top . . . dream images of stones in a circle . . . primordial places of devotion, the sacred grotto . . . attending the Goddess. For modern woman, the circle of stones as the place of centered stillness . . . listening to what is within, her work of individuation as her woman's ego separates from the values around her and finds a ground, through its roots in the Archetypal Feminine, in the sacred Self within.

This writing rests on the image of a circle of stones. Not contiguous, the spaces in between trust the feeling and intuition of the reader to bridge the gaps. The themes—not linear, but circular, like the feminine process of consciousness in either man or woman come round again and again, impressing meaning through nuance, soft change of colouration, shift of light and shadow, repeating, chorus-like, perhaps comfortingly, lulling, soothing, deepening the imprint through subtle change of cadence, rubato.

The underlying theme . . . of woman's birth from woman . . . identification with the Feminine . . . separation, as the animus, her masculine side, exerts its pull . . . her eventual return to feminine ground . . . to come to her own unique consciousness of the Archetypal Feminine . . . to let the strong, wise, and deep Feminine manifest in her life . . . now, not in unconscious identification, but through her own individual, subjective being and efforts.

This is not meant as a primer to instruct in the feminine individuation process, but an intimate testament for a woman to hold in her hand as she finds her own way how, into, and through.

How might your life have been different if there had been a place for you, a place for you to go to be with your mother, with your sisters and the aunts, with your grandmothers, and the great- and great-great-grandmothers, a place of women to go, to be, to return to, as woman?

How might your life be different?

Introduction

Sometimes dreams alter the course of an entire life.

In the summer of my forty-sixth year, one day before my birthday, I had a dream that did not so much alter the course of my life as it did confirm, in the deepest possible way, its pre-existing course—confirm that which my life already, however gropingly, was becoming.

For two years before the dream, a series of images had come to me around the motif of women seated in a circle, coming together to understand their lives. The images had come, wondrously, one by one, each time as I was about to lead a women's group in monthly retreat. Each image began with the words "How might your life have been different if . . ." They named themselves the Circle of Stones.

Into this, then, came the dream. It took that which I cared most deeply about in myself and my work and turned it over slowly and thoughtfully, reflecting various aspects of it and pointing out its validity and meaning. The dream said to me that what I was doing, my life, my ideas, and my work, were coming out of a center inside myself. It said that I needed to trust the truth of that process and to let it come out more fully. I needed to leave behind an allegiance to the collective values in order to trust that which was truly individual, was truly my own, a woman's own, was very much needed.

The dream and images themselves spoke powerfully to me of my life as woman. The women with whom I shared them were moved by them. I thought that they might carry meaning to other women, also. And so I began, tentatively, to write.

This present writing grew, bit by bit, as the dream unfolded and intertwined with the images. As the meaning of one piece, then another, emerged, a configuration began to take shape. It was of a woman separating from her surroundings and letting herself come to birth.

Many times I faltered or held back, through lack of faith or self-doubt. The last link to fall into place was *The Elamites*. I dimly remembered a mention of Elam from childhood Old Testament lessons. This part of the circle was brought 'round when a teacher of Hebrew identified Elam as among the last of lands honouring the feminine Deity, among the last of lands where woman had a voice.

The dream's final scene portrayed a young woman of today newly come to her own voice, newly come to her authority in outer affairs, while remaining grounded in her inner feeling values. It completed the circle.

This writing attempts to reflect the intertwining of the initiating images, the dream, and women's experiencing of them.

self / *Self*

The use of lower case "s" in the word "self" is to indicate the finite sense of self within the individual, already in the child, which will later form a relationship with the transcendent, or infinite, Self. This usage is based on my understanding of the works of C. G. Jung.

in search of Her
MOTHER

Long ago before the patriarchal period, in many places on earth, the Goddess was worshipped. Woman in the train of history has been orphaned by the death of this Great Mother, has suffered loss of connection to her own beingness, lack of sense of legitimacy and belonging in the universe or in her own individual life. Woman can draw comfort from an image of the Great Mother reaching out to her to fulfill and to bring to manifest form in her own individual life that of the Archetypal Eternal Feminine. Woman, with the help of the Great Mother, can leave the collective way to find her own individual way, for somewhere deep inside she knows she must leave to become herself.

The universal importance of woman's tears

I am at a conference leading a small group, as I have done many times in waking life. After it is over, one woman, Pat Fleming, speaks with me about the book used for the group, a history of the Elamites, of "how it was before the patriarchal period." I tell her, "It was during that earlier time that something important was allowed . . . " and she says softly, "Yes, sadness."

Then I say good-bye and leave the conference. (And, in fact, shortly before the dream occurred, I had painfully decided that I must leave a conference which had been an important part of my life for more than ten years.) I kiss Sarah, now ninety years old, on the cheek, and kneel down to gather up my books and records. Someone asks, "Do you notice that each time she says good-bye she kneels down to hide her face so her sadness won't be seen?"

The last scene is in my consultation room. I am in session with a young woman of Middle Eastern heritage, whose father was not only strongly oppressive but used a framework of Freudian psychology and actual accusations of "penis envy" to subdue his daughter. She had struggled, in her work and growth, to reclaim her fine intellect and rational thinking to aid her to fulfill herself as a woman: to have that fine rational thinking function serve her *feeling values, rather than to have it dominate them and force her to live out her life either as a power-driven "son" for her father or as a piece of fluff. At the time of the dream, she was in law school* and *about to be engaged to the man she loved—one whom her father had disapproved.*

In the dream setting, the young woman is sitting in the chair across from me. Standing slightly behind her, in the shadows, is her Middle Eastern grandfather, in his native costume. The air around him is crackling with traditional patriarchal tribal laws, taboos, and mores. It is clear that if he had had his way, neither his grand-daughter nor I would be there, certainly not sitting quietly and conferring about her life and how she intended to live it—claiming her own right to direct it.

The young woman sits and quietly begins to cry.

The grandfather criticizes her tears.

Something of being present in the same room with the two po-larities—the young, emerging, feminine feeling side and the old, negat-ing, oppressing, disapproving patriarchal side—fires my passion and crystallizes my words.

"No!" I say.

"No, she must be allowed to cry. It is only when woman can experience her tears in the moment that she can also experience her true, deep feeling values in the moment. The tears of these young and capable women must be allowed and encouraged to flow—to flow out to the culture and society which so truly and desperately need them and their tears—to help society reconnect with the true and deep values of life which can sustain and support that culture, that life, that of life in their society,

"Someday, when the first woman president of the United States holds the sides of the podium and says 'My fellow Americans . . .' as she is inaugurated, it will be important that she can be there, weeping, as she speaks, and that her tears and the intensity with which she is in

touch with her feeling values can flow out to and nourish the society and influence all women."

When I awoke from the dream, I was amazed at the flow of words and at their passion. It was clear that they had flowed out of my own deepest feeling values—those that I fervently believed in and cared most deeply about.

I was especially touched by the podium scene—as the words "my fellow Americans" were delivered, I had gripped the sides of the lap desk my husband had made for me . . . as if the expression of those deep feeling values from the feminine took place on a platform carefully prepared by the supportive masculine. The dream had reminded me how helpful it is if a woman has support either from an outer man or her own inner masculine side as she brings out her feeling values,

For clearly the values of the feminine need to come forth . . . of the earth, the instincts, the individual . . . all that nurtures and sustains life. Those values need to come forth, to re-emerge with their ancient feminine strength and passion. Those values need to come forth and to voice . . . this time, not to be silenced by the oppressing, negating ancient patriarchy, but to speak clearly and firmly from the even more ancient flow of the Archetypal Feminine.

How might your life have been different if there had been a place for you? A place for you to go . . . a place of women, to help you learn the ways of woman . . . a place where you were nurtured from an ancient flow sustaining you and steadying you as you sought to become yourself. A place of women to help you find and trust the ancient flow already there within yourself . . . waiting to be released . . .

A place of women . . .

How might your life be different?

How it was before . . .

Long ago when life was still sacred, in many places on earth, the Goddess was worshipped. Known by many names in many lands, as Isis, Astarte, Ishtar, Ashtoreth, Hathor, temples built in her honour saw to the care of lands and flocks and kept the books and records.

The Great Goddess was revered in ceremonies perpetuating the fertility and holiness of the earth. Woman crouched on the ground during the menses in rituals regenerating the earth with the flow of her own blood. The gift of sexual love, most sacred of the gifts bestowed by the Goddess, was celebrated in yearly rites as the high priestess or queen of a region united in love with the yearly consort to honour the Goddess. Young women, coming of age, spent a night or more in the temple in sexual union with those coming to pay love honour to the Goddess. Through this act of sexual union, a woman became a virgin . . . sanctified, empowered, and knowing of the mysteries of life.

And, sanctified and empowered unto herself, a woman could empower other women. Woman passed down to woman a sense of herself, of her body, of the mysteries of fecundity and regeneration.

Woman was autonomous, owned property, sat on the councils of elders, served in the courts of law, and passed down the sovereign rule, in many lands, through matrilineal descent. The children born to woman were legitimate and respectable, inheriting her property, name and title, in many places, whether or not she was married. Woman was recognized for her knowledge and sought out for her advice in practical matters. She held jobs alongside men and was valued for her insight and authority in all things seen.

But it was for her insight and authority in things unseen that woman was most valued. Through her feminine rituals, through the sacred act of sexual love, woman came into the direct presence of the Goddess, and through this experience, was opened to her own prophetic and oracular vision.

Woman knew the mysteries of life and how to invoke the primal elements of nature, touchable and untouchable. Woman passed down to woman knowledge of the elemental energies in the earth and in herself, and of how to align herself with the eternal flow of those energies, within and without.

Woman passed down to woman a sense of the Goddess, of the Primal Feminine and her belonging within it. Woman passed down to woman a sense of herself as *"woman unto herself."*

Woman passed down to woman a respect for her own being, revering the Great Mother in herself and herself in the Great Mother.

Woman passed down to woman a way of being within herself as she carried out her daily tasks in which she related to herself and to the task as sacred and necessary to the completion of the cosmic cycle, to be fulfilled by her, by her alone, again and again. Through that fulfilling, she renewed the earth, blessing the cycles of nature, quietly carving into the stillness of time the steps of her repeated trips for water, her winnowing of the grain, her nurturing of the earth.

Time passed.

Things began to change.

Laws were introduced taking rights of inheritance away from woman. Control over her property, finances, and legal affairs was given to the men related to her. Her political and social autonomy was taken, and in some places she was considered property.

The most supreme gift of the Goddess was denigrated —sexual love was shamed and reviled. Her claiming of her sexuality as sacred to herself and to the Goddess was scorned and humiliated. Sexual union, once sacred and ecstatic, became debauchery. The sacred temple rituals, wherein a woman had become holy and free, were condemned as orgiastic and the priestesses as "temple prostitutes."

The sacred groves dedicated to the worship of the Great Mother were condemned and closed. The serpent, venerable symbol of wisdom and nobility, was denigrated and reviled. It became, for the epochs following, a target for humiliation and derision, treated as a symbol of woman's folly, evil, cunning, and lust. This ancient symbol of life was abased as that which tempted Eve, and, through Eve, all of humankind, into sin and death.

The wisdom of woman, gained through her identification with her body, with the Goddess, and with the earth, was no longer revered, but ridiculed and rejected. Once honoured as prophetess and seer, woman was now scorned. Her instincts and intuition, through which she perceived the elemental energies in the cycles of nature and her knowledge of healing, were rebuked and humiliated.

Among the last of nations to hold the Goddess in highest reverence and woman in a place of honour was the small land of Elam. Lying in the Zagros Mountains between the Caspian Sea and the Persian Gulf, Elam was known in the ancient world for the unique respect it gave woman. The right to its royal throne passed down in complex forms of matrilineal succession through much of Elam's history until the capital city Susa, the temple, and the ziggurat were razed (circa 627 B.C.).

In Elam, the snake, ancient symbol of the Goddess and feminine wisdom, was represented in bronze-casting and pottery. The Elamites knew the symbol of the tree of life with its coiling serpent. The fertility symbol of intertwining mating snakes spread through the ancient world.

In Elam, the Great Mother was revered as primary deity. Not until the second millennium B.C. was Her position threatened. And then, even as the Goddess relinquished ever greater worldly authority to the male gods, the secret rites of Elam remained those of the Goddess, the earth, and the serpent.

In Elam, among the last and alone, the Goddess was revered, woman was honoured, and, through the sacred sexual rites, she tended the elemental energies in the cycles of nature, reconsecrating the Goddess, the earth, and her own body.

In Elam, last and alone, woman still passed down to woman entitlement to live her life in devotion to the Goddess and to the feminine within herself.

In Elam, last and alone, woman passed down to woman the sense of living her life each day identifying with the Great Mother, knowing that life was sacred, within and without.

And then in Elam,
in Elam, also, things began to change,
No more could woman hold up her head to
revere the Goddess and honour herself.
No more could woman hold up her head,
No more.
No more.

How it was before . . .

How might it have been different for you, if, on your first menstrual day, your mother had given you a bouquet of flowers and taken you to lunch, and then the two of you had gone to meet your father at the jeweler, where your ears were pierced, and your father bought you your first pair of earrings, and then you went with a few of your friends and your mother's friends to get your first lip colouring;
and then you went,
for the very first time,
to the Women's Lodge,
to learn
the wisdom of the women?

How might your life be different?

"Yes, sadness . . ."

In my dream the woman who spoke of Elam was Pat Fleming. She and I had known one another for half a dozen years through a conference on religion and psychology. Pat was warm and embracing, maternal. A few weeks after she appeared in my dream, her article appeared in *Psychological Perspectives*. In it she wrote of her loss of, and life-long search for, her mother.

The issue published a brief summary of Pat's life . . . and an announcement of her death. Her own mother had died a few hours after Pat's birth, and the daughter had spent her lifetime in search of the lost mother. In the article Pat traced the steps of her earliest infant experiencing of her loss of the mother and her feelings of emptiness as a child. She wrote of her life-long effort to find a connection to an external mother, and her final hard-won sense of self as her dreams grounded her in a mothering source within herself. Pat's writing described poignantly the depth of her own sadness—the black hole within the motherless child.

The mother, first representative of the Self to the infant, constellates in the infant what will become the sense of Self within as the child grows. As the baby sees itself mirrored in the face of the mother, sees its own image lovingly reflected in the mother's eyes, a fledgling sense of a true and worthy self is born within the infant. With the birth of that sense of self is born a sense of being seen, recognized, and valued as who one really is.

Loss of the personal mother may leave the child without sense of self or self-worth, without hope that one will ever be seen as oneself, There is fear of being unable to become one's true self, of never being truly known—never knowing who one truly is. One is left, abandoned, isolated, without hope of future . . . as Pat wrote, floating in "black emptiness."

Loss of the mother is experienced as a totality of loss of safety, security, nurture, comfort, or joy. The child, rather than knowing itself as valued, embraced, and precious, perceives itself as tainted, condemned, sick, shamed, and guilty—eternally unworthy of love. There is a loss of the possibility of being acknowledged as who one most deeply is.

Pat wrote of the daughter's need to separate from and then to introject her mother in order to connect with a source of nurture within herself. If a girl loses her mother and is unable to complete this process, she may live in fantasy, conscious or unconscious, of restoring the original unbroken uruboric connection, the hope of complete unity with the mother. She may go through life endlessly seeking her mother, involved in ceaseless activity, seeing her image in suitable as well as unsuitable individuals, and seeking from them the love and nurture so deeply longed for. She may give love to many, seeking, appropriately and inappropriately, through her giving of mothering, to ease the pain of her own loss. At worst, she may catch herself compulsively forcefeeding nurture to those who neither need nor want it.

For a daughter, the steps of separating and introjecting are necessary so that she may later reconnect with the mother. This time, it will be no longer in an identification, being "just like mommy," but in real relatedness to the mother as other. Now, the daughter may experience her own equal reality and substance as woman. Now, she may become her own individual woman self with a center, a grace and maturity of her own, not eternally a satellite circling an older, stronger woman.

Pat wrote movingly of the comfort she drew from her perception of her search for her mother as that of the daughter Persephone searching for the mother Demeter, even while the mother yearned for and searched for her daughter . . . sought, even as she was seeking . . . each one, the mother as well as the daughter, longing for the love of the other, needing the other's presence, love, reflecting, in order to complete and to fulfill her own feminine life process.

Pat Fleming's story of a daughter's search to recover her mother illustrates, in an individual sense, what the dream image of the Elamites represents in a collective sense: modern woman's search for the Archetypal Mother and her sadness at the loss of all that the death of the mother represents. Just as the daughter needs to mourn and to release the personal mother in order to introject her and come into a new relationship with her, so must women, since the Elamites, mourn and release the Great Mother in order to come to a new relationship and understanding of Her and of themselves as women.

Like Pat, who never had a chance to know her personal mother, woman in the train of history has had little chance to know her collective Great Mother and has longed to regain and know Her. Woman in the train of history, orphaned by the death of the Great Mother, has suffered loss of connection to her own beingness, lack of sense of legitimacy and belonging in the universe or in her own individual life. Orphaned, woman has been treated as orphan. She has received shame and humiliation, has felt unworthy of love and dignity. Full of self-loathing, she has put herself and other women last.

"Yes, sadness . . ."

Woman, so unmothered, has not had a chance to separate from, or to introject, the Great and Wise Mother, to feel within herself the possibility of being her own source of nurture, of wisdom. She has remained, often, the eternal girl, unable to feel or claim her full weight, substance, stature.

Woman, so unmothered, needs a chance to mourn her collective loss—to face into the pain of her black emptiness and to release it. She needs to mourn, to let go, in order that she may finally connect inwardly with what she never outwardly had. This lack is not a lack or loss of nurture from a personal mother, but a greater loss—the loss of rootedness and strength flowing in an immense, ancient cord throughout history from the primeval Great Mother Herself.

Woman, so unmothered, needs to connect within with a rootedness, substance, and strength that can ground her and fill her with a sense of what she was, is, and may become. Each woman needs to come to new awareness of her own womanhood, taking care not to fall into unconscious identification with the awesome primal power of the Great Mother or to seek fusion with Her, with the heady inflation that it may bring. Each woman must go through the slow process of discovering who she is and of bringing her self to birth, living in relationship to the Great Mother, but feeling her own personal separateness, her own equal reality—being of the same, but not the same as the Mother—and bringing her own individual life to manifest form in a way that expresses the power, substance, and wisdom of the Archetypal Feminine within herself.

And, as Pat Fleming drew comfort from her perception of Persephone searching for the mother, even while Demeter searched for her daughter, so may women now draw comfort from the image of their Great Mother, in a symbolic and archetypal sense, searching for Her lost daughters in today's tangled world.

Woman may draw comfort from an image of the Great Mother reaching out Her arms to Her daughters, yearning for them—longing to reconnect, to sustain and encourage them, to offer solace, strength, and wisdom as they fulfill their lives . . . an image of the Great Mother needing Her daughters, needing each one to fulfill and bring to manifest form in her own individual life that of the Archetypal Eternal Feminine that bore her.

Woman can reconnect with an image of the Great Mother and herself, not as saccharine or sentimentalized, but as clear-eyed, firm, stalwart, straightforward, and steadfast . . . an image of woman mothering her children, mothering herself, rooted in her own strength, substance, and wisdom, rooted, *through her own life*, in the strength, substance, and wisdom of the Eternal Mother.

"Yes, sadness . . ."

How might your life have been different, if, deep within, you carried an image of the Great Mother? And, when things seemed very, very bad, you could imagine that you were sitting in the lap of the Goddess,
held tightly . . .

embraced, at last

And, that you could hear Her saying to you,
"I love you . . .

I love you and I *need* you to bring forth your self."

And, if, in that image, you could see the Great Mother looking to Her daughters, looking to each woman to reveal, in her own life, the beauty, strength, and wisdom of the Mother . . .

How might your life be different?

Then, saying goodbye . . .

In the dream as I was leaving the conference, I kissed Sarah on the cheek. Sarah was loving and faithful. She was a woman of strong religious convictions in the traditional sense. She took as her task leading her life in the imitation of Christ's holiness rather than trying to live out her own wholeness as Christ lived out His.

In waking life Sarah was sixty-five, but in my dream she looked ninety years old, a full and abundant life span. Sarah was greatly loved. She had served the conference prominently for many years, found her niche, and been faithful in service "till the end of her days." How rich and how blessed!

My own alienation and fears stood in stark contrast. I was leaving behind a place of nurture and safety—for the conference had been a deeply nourishing experience for me. I was forced to face myself, my task, my life. Leaving any possibility of serving devotedly with recognition "till the end of my days." And, as in the dream, "she kneels down to hide her face, so her sadness won't be seen," I was leaving with great sorrow, even though I knew I could not grow into myself if I remained.

Leaving behind hearkening to outer authority to find my own meaning. Leaving the clarity and comfort of having my duty defined from outside. Leaving behind projecting my leadership ability onto others instead of owning it myself. Leaving behind being a "good woman" in service to others. Forced, now, to claim my energy to serve the Self as I interpreted it. Forced to become, on my own terms, who I truly was, to be willing to suffer my guilt against the collective for becoming myself.

I was leaving the sister roles of Martha and Mary, the disciples of Christ. Leaving the Martha role of meeting others' needs and the Mary role of listening outside herself for the voice of the Self. I was leaving to attend the voice within, and in the anguish of leaving, a nervous giggle, helpful in its honesty, pointed to my failure in the Martha role . . . rarely had I played it with a truly loving spirit.

I was leaving, for I knew that if a woman in her middle years cannot gather herself to leave the collective way, but clings, through old obedience or loyalty, to outer authority, serving group values in her customary ways, the results would almost surely be negative. There may be a stagnation in her feelings as her service becomes stale and forced, no longer joyously performed from a full heart, but from a tired sense of duty. If she forces herself to continue to serve congregation, community, or family, perhaps even increases her efforts in order to compensate the loss of true heart-devotion, her service may be marked by excess: too many organizational meetings, too many church suppers, too many sweet desserts served, as she pours out, in a displacement, the energy that could flow to attend the Self within.

Finally, she may find herself devoured by envy and jealousies as she sees other women allowing themselves to leave their service to the collective and bring themselves to individual birth. She will resent that they allow themselves to be what she has not allowed herself to become. For somewhere deep inside, she knows that she must leave to become herself.

How might your life have been different if there had been a place for you . . . a place of women, where you were received and affirmed? A place where other women, perhaps somewhat older, had been affirmed before you, each in her time, affirmed, as she struggled to become more truly herself.

A place where, after the fires were lighted, and the drumming, and the silence, there would be a hush of expectancy filling the entire chamber . . . a knowing that each woman there was leaving old conformity to find her self . . . a sense that all of womanhood stood on a threshold.

And if, during the hush, the other women, slightly older, had helped you to trust your own becoming . . . to trust it and quietly and prayerfully to nurture it . . .

How might your life be different?

Woman, standing on a hillside, peering,

peering into blue space . . .

. . . what will woman be?

. . . not yet fully seen

. . . not yet fully revealed

. . . but coming

. . . coming

. . . what will woman be?

in search of Her

SELF

To discover who she is, a woman must descend into her own depths. She must leave the safe role of remaining a faithful daughter of the collectives around her and descend to her individual feeling values. It will be her task to experience her pain . . . the pain of her own unique feeling values calling to her, pressing to emerge. To discover who she is, a woman must trust the places of darkness where she can meet her own deepest nature and give it voice . . . weaving the threads of her life into a fabric to be named and given . . . sharing it with the women around her as she comes to a true and certain sense of herself.

A sense of her depth

Years before . . .

A woman in a laundromat, on a busy street in a large, industrial city stood smoothing the towels and bedding as she spread them on the folding table. With her hand, over and over, smoothing out each piece, smoothing out the wrinkle from the center towards the edges, smoothing further, further until the fabric lay wholly smooth, flat, a still, unruffled surface.

A younger woman watched . . .

Years passed.

A woman in her kitchen, pouring tea slowly into cups standing in a circle on a round tray . . . slowly . . . slowly . . . listening to the sound of the liquid as the cups filled . . . a slender stream of fragrant steaming tea . . . knowing that each woman waiting in the next room in a small circle listened, each one, also, as the tea was poured, knowing that the quietness of the pouring and the warmth of the cups held between each pair of hands made a difference, was somehow important . . . knowing that this moment and this way of living out this moment was significant . . . that it made a difference in the meaning and experiencing of life.

A difference in the experiencing of life . . . a woman pouring tea, knowing this difference, trusting the knowing, enabled, by her trust, to pour even more slowly. . . listening to the tranquilly flowing liquid . . . listening . . . listening . . .

a woman in her kitchen . . .

A woman, searching for her self, must descend to her own depths. She must leave the upper world of people and events, her old safe role of faithful daughter to collective values in the society around her, and descend to her own feeling values.

She must descend, alone, to the still, dark realm of the unformed, the inchoate, to the chasm of her own void . . . descend, silently into the murky, formless, half earth, half water depths . . . into a damp, echoing cavern, to sit and wait for that of her self which cannot be met in the upper world.

As she first descends, she may sense only the void. The conventions of her upbringing may not allow her to witness the pain and isolation within. Her task will be to witness her own pain . . . the pain of her subjective values crying out to her, pressing to emerge. She must bring those values to clarity and expression in the patterns of her daily life.

As she descends, a woman touches a strength, a certainty that changes her. Once encountering that dark chasm within, she can no longer ignore her own experience, her own pain. She can no longer live her life in an easy way, dovetailing with the collective.

Her knowledge of her own depth, the intensity of feeling contained within, forces her to a new stance . . . a stance that is subjective and unique, mirroring the anguish of each individual struggling to come to birth . . . struggling against the established order . . . against that which is already given and known.

Each woman must come to a new valuing of her own process in its diffuse, structureless ineffability. She must see that her process is as much needed for wholeness as the masculine process, which, with its clarity, definition, logic, and order, has so often seemed the superior.

A woman, grounded in the Yin, because of the differing nature of Yin from Yang, is faced with an eternal paradox. The nature of Yin, receptive, is to yield. The nature of Yang is to press forward, to dominate. Yet the two are forever intrinsically equal. And, like shadow and light, each needs the other to delineate and complete its existence.

As a woman descends to her feeling depths, she touches a separate mode of being. It is grounded in the Archetypal Feminine and, through it, in the eternal Self. In her descent, a woman strikes root in that Self.

She returns to the world changed.

How might your life have been different if there had been a place for you to be, a place of women . . . a place where, one day in your monthly stay, you were asked if it were almost time? And, if other women, somewhat older, already initiated, had begun to help you prepare?

And, for many months, the women helped you during your times in the lodge to go inside yourself and consider all the experiences of your life and to reflect on them . . . if the women had helped you draw your thoughts and feelings together and to weigh them . . . So that you could come to a clearer knowing of what your life was about. And if the women had listened as you told them of your whole life and the sense and meaning it held for you . . . the happenings of your whole life.

And, at the end of that process, after the bathing and fasting, and praying . . . the oldest women in the lodge had come and sat in a circle, and you saw that they had left an empty place . . . a place for you. And you softly and timidly made your way to the empty place and quietly claimed your wisdom, the wisdom of your soul . . .

How might your life be different?

A *sense of her feelings*

Derisive voices: *Crybaby! Stupid female! Turn it off!* Her sorrow, her anger, her pain shamed and ridiculed, woman learned to distrust her feelings, the truth of her existence. She learned to ignore, deny, suppress them, until they became repressed. She hardened herself to her own suffering as society became hardened to the suffering of humanity, crushed in the dehumanization of mass culture, mass production, mass conflict.

Woman has learned to ignore her own feeling needs, learned to be a "good sport" hurrying along in a pressure-filled, production-oriented life. She has learned to brush her feelings aside as she pushes ahead for university honours, to pack them out of her briefcase as she heads, in a three-piece suit, into the professional and political realm.

> *But somewhere, deep inside, is the image of a woman*
> *seated alone, in a beehive tomb,*
> *within the earth,*
> *weeping.*

What if woman allowed herself to listen once again to her own sensitivities? To listen to the ways in which she is unhappy? What if she allowed herself to trust what her tears are trying to tell her?

"No . . . not this way . . .
No . . . your life has no meaning lived this way.
No . . .
No . . .
Slow down.
Rest,
Fill the kettle slowly.
Listen! as the water in its slender stream
flows down to fill the waiting kettle."

A woman, age 55, speaks of her struggle:

"Oh, the time, the endless pressure of time. Even when I have a whole day, I still can't get to my own things—I don't even know what they are . . .

"I vacuum, do the bookkeeping . . . always production-oriented . . . the endless realm of keeping busy . . . when I was young, my mother always expected us to keep busy . . . she couldn't imagine my need to have time for myself . . . if one of her daughters would be a bit quiet or inward one day, she would right away immediately accuse us of being lazy and give us a task to do.

"In my dreams there is a quiet chamber, an inner corridor for which I'm always searching and can never quite get to . . . a quiet, dark place . . . where I'm allowed to just sit . . . alone . . . and be still."

What if a woman were to allow herself to trust her own unhappiness and to make life changes—changes that would allow time and place for her to experience her life as it lives itself out *slowly*, moment by moment? To allow herself time and place to be present to her own burning fire, the water springing from the rock of her own experience . . . to allow herself to leave behind the jet plane, the express lane, and simply to *be*, there, for a moment, present to her own life?

What if a woman trusted her own tears enough to listen to them, to make real changes in her individual schedule, and to see if those changes spread to her office, her committee, her religious group?

What if she trusted her anger, her irritation, her illness, even her depression, as signs that her own life was calling to her?

What if a woman allowed herself to leave a mode of doing that does not nourish her, that actively makes her unhappy? What if it were not so difficult? If her upbringing had not sought to teach her to be dutiful, moral, caring, giving, helpful, productive and loving . . . at all times . . . to all others.

A woman dreamed:

> *"I am standing on a large map, on the paper itself, somewhere in upstate New York, where my parents' people come from. Others are with me on one of the thick red lines that are the superhighways on the map.*
>
> > *We go back and forth*
> > *. . . back and forth . . .*
> > *back and forth.*
> > *It is pointless . . .*
> > *and endless.*
>
> *Finally I leave the red-line superhighway.*

A sense of her feelings

I go to a very faint little dotted line, not very clearly marked on the map . . . hardly more than a footpath, really. The map shows only the beginning of the road, not where it will lead. It is scary because it is so narrow and winding, not clearly marked.

I worry that I should have done the approved thing and stayed on the big road with all the others. But I see that here I am closer to the trees, which I have loved all my life, and which are very important to me."

This woman, in her mid-sixties, had recently retired from her career as a special-education teacher. It had been an exhausting, albeit fulfilling job, and she was struggling to claim her life and the passage of her time for herself. Her upbringing, which emphasized charity to others rather than to oneself, still gripped her strongly. It left her always conflicted between enrolling for yet another course to enable her to give "more and better to others" or finally allowing herself to hear her own needs for rest and reflection.

Her deepest longing, to attend to the Self, was fulfilled only with great guilt. Long after it had become clear to her that she no longer wished to continue in her familial patterns, she found herself still taking on service work in her religious meeting and registering for study in a caregiving curriculum.

The persistent Self, in its faithfulness to her, managed to get her attention in one of the only ways left to it as she proceeded on her path of doing good in the collective realm. It appeared at the cellular level in the form of a sharp physical pain . . . and, as she called it, "a pain in the seat, at that."

It attacked and awakened her out of sleep at night. Its insistence impressed itself upon her as a fearsome friend. Over the months, the persistence of the pain coincided more and more clearly with situations in which she had ignored the voice of the Self within and had followed her old pattern of outer, rather than inner, listening and serving. She learned to trust the pain as helper—a helper which gripped her each time she did not listen to her true Self. Gradually, whenever the pain came, she would examine what she had been doing in waking life, to see in what ways she had made "the same old choices to serve others and to betray my own needs," and then to change those choices.

The dream of the superhighway was confirming and clarifying to her. It helped her to know that her own unconscious recognized the difficulty of her struggle, and affirmed that she was, indeed, at last able to leave the superhighway of her very moral ancestors and to find her own path.

Her physical pain had forced her to recognize her dilemma and to give herself permission to move towards change.

It is often, finally, a woman's own pain and sadness that make her change her life. Finally it is impossible to deny her feelings any longer.

How might it have been different for you, if, early in your life, the first time you as a tiny child felt your anger coming together inside yourself, someone, a parent or grandparent, or older sister or brother, had said, "Bravo! Yes, that's it! You're feeling it!"

If, the first time you had experienced that sharp awareness of ego, of "me, I'm *me,* not you" . . . you had been received and hugged and affirmed, instead of shamed and isolated?

If someone had been able to see that you were taking the first tiny baby step towards feeling your own feelings, of knowing that you saw life differently from those around you. If you had been helped to experience your own uniqueness, to feel the excitement of sensing, for the very first time, your own awareness of life. What if someone had helped you to own all of this . . . to own your own life?

How might it be different for you?

A *sense of her process*

If a woman is trapped in a collective framework, unable, because of family or economic pressure, to give time to herself, her need for rescue may fall to the unconscious, and its response may come in the form of a depression.

Sometimes, into the lives of women who seem to be successfully fulfilling the standards of the surrounding society, depression may come as a settling embrace. It may come to a woman who is terrified that there will be nothing there, inside, if she allows herself time to rest, to separate from her extraverted hyperactivity in the outer world. Or it may come to a woman who already vaguely senses a different way, a more elemental mode than she is living out. Perhaps she has dimly glimpsed a way, more in touch with herself and life, that would reflect more truly her own feelings and life values. Yet she has chosen as she has chosen. Her choices may have seemed better, safer, all she was able to do at the time.

The old story: unable to leave behind that which one has been taught is sensible, practical, normal, rational, proper, decent convention. Better to regard the group over the individual, the publicly acclaimed over the privately treasured, the objective over the subjectively valued.

Into such a life, depression comes as a gift, bringing the chance to strike root in a deeper ground inside oneself. Depression comes as a gift forcing one to listen to the voice of the Self within.

Depression comes as a gift wrenching one from the comfort of the collective to the isolation of one's own feeling values, from the safety of the wide gate and broad way to the doubts and fears of one's own unmarked, rocky footpath . . . a gift: for hidden in the seeming safety of the broad way was stagnation and illness—death to the possibility of becoming oneself.

Depression comes as a gift that stops one from hurrying briskly, confidently into the market. Stops one from rushing to the shopping center to buy one more bargain blouse for an already overcrowded closet. Stops one from emptily mouthing what one no longer believes in anyway.

Depression stops time

. . . and one settles into one's own waters as a sailing vessel without wind . . . without wind . . . without momentum . . . and one sinks into one's depths.

And somewhere, deep inside, in the beehive tomb,
    . . . one sits alone
        . . . and weeps.

Depression comes as a gift asking that a woman recognize her own substance and trust it as the quiet, steady voice of her own truth. As she trusts it, hearkens to it, attends as it unfolds, she learns that of herself never allowed to develop when her allegiance was with the collective.

She learns that of herself
    . . . never allowed to live
        . . . nor helped to speak.

Depression serves a woman as it presses down on her, forcing her to leave behind that which was not of herself, which had influenced her to live a life alien to her own nature. Her suffering, now substantial, insists that she no longer deny its truth. She can no longer "keep a stiff upper lip," or "pack up her troubles in her old kit bag and smile, smile, smile," or, as one woman struggling with her weight said, "rise above it all." These phrases were said with harsh smiles and self-condemning voices by three women who had castigated themselves for being unable to deny depression. Now, each woman was facing her own pain, seeking to simply be within it, each trusting her own darkness to reveal her truth.

"I had to give up my old idea of who I was . . . all my old beliefs. Finally I was ground to a halt.

"All the enthusiastic bustle . . . it all ceases . . . one drops into an abyss . . . nothingness . . . black emptiness . . .

time itself warps . . .

slows . . .

seems to stop."

In an absence of happenings, the realm of matter fills one's senses . . . smells, sounds, textures. At last there is time enough to be with one's surroundings.

"I sat in the wicker chair near the window . . .
a raindrop ran slowly . . .
one single raindrop . . .
very large . . .
down the pane of glass . . .
all the way to the bottom of the window.
It sat there for a little while.
Then another drop started at the top of the pane.
It was very comforting."

A sense of her process

With the humbling of the old ego position comes a slowing of awareness that allows one to notice, wordlessly, one's left hand . . . warmed by the cup held in it . . . the fingers on the right . . . cramped from the handle of the cup.

Time . . .
   Time . . .
      The infinitesimally slow passage of time.
        . . . from microsecond
          . . . to microsecond
            . . . to microsecond.
. . . from the first fluttering flakes,
   through an eternal night
     of silent,
       softly falling snow . . .
         Stillness.

Depression asks that the attitude towards one's life be changed, that the source of authority be recognized as no longer outside, but now deeply within, that one relate to each event, task, and moment of one's life personally, subjectively.

Depression demands that one's life be viewed, no longer objectively, as time or energy available to be spent in service to external authority, be it religious, state, professional, or even family, but to be held sacred, and lived, moment by moment, as one's own.

How might your life have been different, if, when you were a young woman, the first time you felt feelings of depression, an older woman had come to sit with you? If she had come to sit with you, as someone had come to sit with her the first time she had feelings of depression? To simply sit, quietly, perhaps wordlessly—to sit with you, during your dark time

And how might your life have been different if the woman had accepted your feelings of depression? Had accepted them so completely and fully that you began to feel safe with them. If there had been no judgement and no questioning . . . no attempt to make you smile, to betray your feelings, to deny your darkness. If the woman had simply sat in silence with you, with your pain, and in the darkest moments had been able to reflect it to you . . . to reflect to you your pain . . . to witness . . . attend . . . and by her quiet respect for it to help you learn to respect it . . . your own pain and depression . . . to witness, attend and respect your depression . . . and to see that just as the woman had faith in it, you also might have a glimmer of faith that there was meaning and truth in your darkness.

How might your life be different?

A *sense of her fear*

Present-day society is afraid of depression. Whatever it resembles—reflection, introversion, a drawing within for quietness—may also be feared. In the past, the Orient had a place for the individual to withdraw, a closet in the household for solitude, for nurture of the Yin, to counterbalance the Yang energy necessary for outer life. But present-day Occidental attitudes esteem energetic, enthusiastic extraversion and exert pressure on the individual to exhibit it almost exclusively. Suffering is feared and the sufferer outcast. Collective attitudes have evolved fostering archetypal masculine doing and achievement values. As woman entered the work realm outside her home, there was little alternative but to adopt those values. There was little recognition that her process as woman was of a different nature or that doing/achievement values were not complete or valid for her.

The issue is not whether woman can achieve, but that preoccupation with achievement may deny a descent into her deeper nature which a woman must make to touch her true strengths. The masculine must perhaps fly to fulfill a part of its heroic nature. But woman, pressed to fly, may lose herself and be prevented from descending into her depths, prevented from fulfilling her own feminine nature. For through her descent, she touches the power of the feminine, a power that comes of *being,* not *doing* . . . the power of wisdom in the face of a very old woman, a face on which one reads, "I know what I know."

A woman, through her descent, touches a deeply feminine authority, as different from the authority of the masculine as is the moon from the sun.

It is an authority not of abstracted, rational, objective knowledge, but an authority which allows her to speak from her own unique experiencing of life, from her own deepest personal conviction.

A woman, prevented by her own fears or cultural attitudes from making this descent, is left to speak only from her achievement-oriented side rather than from a deeper experiencing of herself as woman. Because present-day society has not understood, has feared the process which woman must undergo to claim her power and wisdom, has recognized only the masculine process, women have been left little alternative but to speak "as men." Speaking, then, out of their lesser side, they have appeared strident, pompous, or dominated by the masculine aspects of themselves.

Woman herself has become alienated from her need to sink into herself. She has begun to expect herself to have the energies, emotions, and attitudes of the masculine. It is a tragic token of the lack of recognition of a separate and unique feminine process that, the more intelligent and educated a woman is, the more she may feel that she has been asked to alienate herself from her deeper feminine nature. Not only her professional commitment, but her specific job, social position, and family may seem to forbid her finding and striking root in the power and authority of the Archetypal Feminine. Because her descent is not understood and not valued, woman has difficulty embracing a distinctly feminine wisdom and power. Society has been the poorer: a uniquely feminine authority, in its fully developed forms, has been absent.

The result is that a woman descending into her deeper nature does not speak about it if she wishes to remain socially acceptable. Several important losses occur to herself and her society. First, she does not hear from her own voice what she experienced and learned of her own life values in the descent. She gains neither her wisdom nor her voice.

Second, there is no chance for one woman's descent to serve as comfort and guide for others during their own descent. The experience of one already initiated is disregarded, never allowed to instruct and succor the neophyte. A woman is robbed of the surety that her suffering will have meaning or serve purpose for another.

Third, and most important in a collective sense, is that all that has been learned in the descent, the accumulated wisdom of woman after woman, gets lost. Since the process by which the wisdom comes to birth is held invalid, the wisdom itself, born of that process, is also invalidated, not allowed to emerge or to speak. A woman could be helped to understand her depression as a passage of initiation to claim her own soul and wisdom to be shared, later, with other women as they prepare for their own passage. She is taught, instead, to fear her experience and to loathe herself.

At the individual level, a woman who could be helped by simply hearing another woman's experience of her descent and the understanding of it that came during and after it, has, instead, only a void, "an empty blackness." The words bringing greatest comfort to one in suffering, those expressing the anguish and re-emergence of another, are not spoken or preserved. Those words . . . words sharing suffering in its passage through pain, darkness, anger, fear, and alienation . . . those words need to be spoken. Those words of suffering, following a passage like an underground river slowly winding its way, and finally days and nights later turning towards the light . . . those words need to be shared with the renewed life and meaning the sufferer has found in the process.

It is this meaning, found by a woman in her suffering, that will sustain the initiate during her own descent. It is this meaning, emerged from her own suffering, that allows a woman to descend, each time anew, into her own depths, to be present to the truth and wisdom lying there. For only by her *willing* descent can she uncover, again and again, the meaning of her life.

Can we come to a new understanding of the feminine process towards wholeness? Can we, as women, take it upon ourselves to deepen within ourselves and each other an appreciation of the descent in the feminine process?

How might your life have been different, if, as a young woman, there had been a place for you, a place where you could go to be among women . . . a place for you when you had feelings of darkness? And, if there had been another woman, somewhat older, to be with you in your darkness, to be with you until you spoke . . . spoke out your pain and anger and sorrow.

And, if you had spoken until you had understood the sense of your feelings, how they reflected your own nature, your own deepest nature, crying out of the darkness, struggling to be heard.

And, what if, after that, every time you had feelings of darkness, you knew that the woman would come to be with you? And would sit quietly by as you went into your darkness to listen to your feelings and bring them to birth . . . So that, over the years, companioned by the woman, you learned to no longer fear your darkness, but to trust it . . . to trust it as the place where you could meet your own deepest nature and give it voice.

How might your life be different if you could trust your darkness . . . could trust your own darkness?

A sense of her need

If a woman is caught in overextended lifestyle and achievement-oriented values, depression or illness may offer the only opportunity to allow her to be with herself. As she ignores her own needs for quiet and self-nurture, the voice of the deeper Self may call through depression. If a woman cannot let herself hear her own needs, but continues to adhere fearfully to a lifestyle that denies her inner growth and deepening, the voice of the Self may manifest in physical illness as the only possible way to force her to take time to be with herself. The more she is trapped in a competitive mode, the more likely the inner voice will manifest at the physical level—*it will be heard!*

The fears a woman may have before leaving the competitive mode may rage for a long time and make her defend dogmatically the activities that a deeper part of her already dimly senses are harming her. As she struggles towards a new choice, she may not know where to turn for support.

A woman speaks of her experience with illness:

"Part of what kept me in the professional world for so long was fear of what my women friends would say if I quit. They were all successful in their fields and disapproved copping-out for any reason. When they were sick, they were worse than any male boss in expecting themselves to overcome . . . like drill sergeants . . . even with their children.

"How harmful is the old slogan 'look like a woman, think like a man, work like a horse.' We expect ourselves always to be Amazons, with all the emphasis on achieving, on appearing 'all right' rather than on the basic stuff of life . . . the sense of protectedness and safety, the warmth, nurture, caring that we all so desperately need.

"I was most afraid of what my mother would say. She hadn't had the educational opportunity she wanted. I despaired being a failure in her eyes or the eyes of my women friends. I solved the problem for myself by getting cancer.

"It wasn't that I needed a free afternoon occasionally, as friends suggested. My whole life had to change. It needed to be claimed for myself . . . all of it . . . I needed to stop living my life in bondage, stealing furtive moments here and there to <u>be</u>.

"My fear of not being seen as successful died hard. Only when I was faced, a second time, with losing my life, could I begin to care for it and for my right to live it enough to really claim it . . . to really claim it for myself in ways I didn't know anything about, at first. Every part of my life had to change . . . most importantly, the way I treated myself.

"The way we women treat ourselves is shocking . . . working long hours, rushing to the market, driving home in traffic. You sometimes see a woman slap her child across the face in the supermarket . . . always the weakest and most vulnerable take the punishment. The advertising and the inner pressure to compete goad us . . . a long workday, then barging into the kitchen, food processor, microwave, all the machines roaring at once. What a shame! . . . a loaf of bread that might have been quietly kneaded and left to rise in the sunshine by the kitchen window . . . now it is slammed out by machine after the woman has worked all day and before she goes to an evening meeting.

"In that earlier life I was always proving, proving that I could. It is as if my cells couldn't stand the way I was living. They demanded that my whole life change. I see how separated I was from myself! I didn't know any more what I needed or how to live. I took myself completely for granted and assumed I knew, like a mother sometimes treats her child, thinking she is a wonderful mother, assuming she knows what's best, never giving the child time enough to feel or choose or speak.

"At first I just sat around in a state of shock, staring at the wall. There wasn't energy for anything but the special diet and what needed to be done right then to stay alive. Looking back, that was the only way to start . . . to just stare at the wall. Finally, finally my life slowed down enough to let the assumptions that had driven it all those years fall away.

"I began to take care of my body, my tired cells, and I slept. I let myself sleep, for the first time in my adult life. Sometimes, when the old guilt would nag me, I would imagine the voice of a kindly old nurse I once knew saying, 'There, there, dear. You just wrap yourself up in this old quilt and have a nap.' And I did, in front of the fireplace, lying in the winter sun.

"Now I take walks and sit in the garden, Now there is time. I listen to my inner child and my outer little girl. They are both happier. Now we all may live."

Illness forces one to care for oneself at the most elemental level, that of matter itself. In illness, no choice remains but to care for the body, to be caring to the cells. In illness, finally, comes permission to rest, permission to treat with love and kindness the base matter of one's own body.

"I could move only . . . so slowly . . . only a few steps at a time. I would spend long hours sitting in a chair.

"There was a comforter over my legs. I cared about that comforter. It was important to me . . . I needed it. It was light blue with a little white flower design, frayed at the top edge, near the row of cloth buttons. It was heavy and warm, and it tucked snugly around my legs into the big chair.

"I sat at the window by the garden, watching the birds at the feeder. We had a simple relationship, the birds and I . . . they ate . . . I watched.

"Time passed.

"In the afternoon . . . late . . . the light changed. I watched the bare tree branches. The wind dropped. Everything was quite still . . . darker.

"It had been a long time since I had watched a star come out."

How might your life have been different, if, deep within, ever since you were a little girl, you carried an image of an old nursemaid, a simple, large woman, comfortable in her substantiality . . . a woman in a rocking chair who nurtured in a gentle, elemental way, who provided an ample lap to crawl up into . . . warm, full arms to hold you . . . and a mellow, throaty voice that said, as she rocked:

"There, there, now. There, there.

"Oh, all those tears, yes. You feel so bad.

"Oh. Oh. Oh.

"All those tears . . .

"You just cry it out. Cry it all out. We'll just sit here and rock while you cry it out. That's it. That's it.

"There. There. There.

Let's put this sweater 'round you. There. There."

A voice to hum, to croon while you cried out all your tears and were comforted. A voice that said, still rocking: *"It's going to be all right. You just have a good cry. Yes, it's going to be all right. We're just going to sit here and rock till you feel better. You just cry it all out till it's better."*

And rocking

Stroking

"There, there, now. There, there.

"Aye, aye, aye.

"There, there now. There, there."

How might your life be different?

A sense of her self

The attitudes of the last historical epoch saw life as pre-ordained. Each day, each moment, was a given, known and directed from above. Little openness remained. Life was to be lived according to all-encompassing codes handed down by divine decree ordering the totality of existence.

But if a woman feels that her life is ordered by another, she cannot relate primarily to her moments and her days. She becomes stifled and strangled. To feel alive, she must reclaim her life, moment by moment, as her own.

A woman must break out of the old mold. She must risk disobeying the given decrees, those dictated from outside as well as those written within her by her past. She must confront her internalized patriarchs and break out of the role of good girl, good woman that they have scripted for her. She must submit to the dread that breaking the old commandments will bring.

A woman must prevail against her guilt and be willing to suffer it as the price she must pay for her freedom. She must undergo the judgement and shaming by her internalized patriarchs again and again—each time reclaiming one small particle of her life as her own.

Only by prevailing against her guilt and dread can a woman bring her life situations, one by one, under her own jurisdiction and authority. Only by prevailing can she relate to her life through her own wisdom and understanding.

As her life comes slowly under her own ken, a woman comes to her own grounding, a sense of her own substance . . . a sureness,

 . . . a steadfastness in herself and her life.

❖ ❖ ❖

In the heat of a late August afternoon . . . four women . . . each seated alone . . . each writing of her understanding of her own life.

The first, a woman strikingly beautiful, already well into the midst of her life, wrote in a letter:

> *"I work very slowly. This has always been a source of great anxiety to me. On this research project I'd hoped to be much further along by this time; had hoped, I suppose, to have accomplished twice as much.*
>
> *"Just recently, however, I may have edged over into a new way of thinking about this. I was asked to review a book for a new publication that will concentrate on women writers. The book seemed so allied to my interests that I felt it would be good to make that kind of digression. Besides, it had been a long time since I reviewed a book, and the thought of doing so again gave me pleasure. So I accepted and then began to have anxiety attacks about how long it was taking. How long should it take to write a review, I kept asking myself.*

"And then it suddenly came to me that the point was not how long should it take, but how long does it take me? I began to make a mental note of how much time I was spending reading, working through each draft, and came up at the end with an approximate number of hours.

"I found the experience very settling. For the first time I had some kind of yardstick by which I could measure the amount of time I would need to set aside for a project of that kind.

"Imagine! Armed with that insight, then I began to think about the length of time I had needed to present an acceptable draft of that initial chapter, how much time I was needing to complete a presentable draft of the current chapter, how much time, therefore, I could expect to need for subsequent chapters . . . The upshot is that I have been able to work out an approximate time for the project, being generous with time allowances and knowing that I will be doing all this within the framework of teaching and whatever else turns up in my life.

"This seems like a very tiny insight, just rephrasing the question: not how long should, but how long does; but I have found it immensely comforting."

The second woman, somewhat younger, recovered from a deep depression, wrote:

"It finally feels as if I am finding my way to my own life. In the quietness I now allow myself to take each morning, I realize that this life is mine . . . finally. It has taken me a long time to know that and to unearth it from under all that buried it . . . it is mine and I care deeply about it . . . I am beginning to understand the meaning of the words 'to cherish.' There is a hush, a sense of waiting . . . as I watch my life unfold itself to me newly each day and beckon me onward to its unfoldment.

"I willingly and lovingly bear the responsibility for it and for myself."

The third woman, still younger, a mother and painter, wrote:

"I want to live my life, my very own life. I want to claim it and live out every particle of it. I hate the possibility of living out a canned version of everybody else's life. Sometimes I have to be frighteningly rebellious because it scares me so to think I won't find out who I am or how to live my life. I worry if a teacher shows my child 'the one and only correct method' to do something and insists that all the children do it that way instead of letting each child discover her or his own method.

"The most dreadful idea in the world for me is that there is a preordained ideal way to live and that we all must live that way. I would rather die than live by a preconceived pattern . . . It would be death in life."

❖ ❖ ❖

The fourth woman reflected on the feelings of the other three, then went on to write of her own experience:

"Once I had an old Oriental teacher.

"I asked him how he did a special sequence the correct way. He, in return, asked me how I did it.

"Six times I asked him, please, to show me how he did it.

"Six times, in return, he asked the same of me.

"By the seventh time, I awakened to what he was telling me.

"I will never forget learning, ever so slowly, that sequence, as it emerged from me.

"No one had ever let that happen before.

"I would like to live my life that way."

How might your life have been different, if, long ago when you were still a tiny child, long before you began to come to the Women's Lodge as the normal cycle of your life, you had been brought here especially by your mother and aunts . . . and you and your girl cousin entered shyly into this place you had overheard so much about?

And, after the fires were lighted, and the drumming, and the silence, you heard, for the very first time, what the women called the Naming . . . each woman speaking slowly into the stillness, sharing her feeling of how she saw her life and what she wished to say of it . . . sharing it with the women around her . . . weaving the threads of her life into a fabric to be given and named.

And, as the shadows of the day lengthened into dusk and you leaned your head against your mother's shoulder, you pondered in your heart a different sense of a woman's life . . .

How might your life be different?

Woman, standing on a hillside, peering, peering into blue space . . .

. . . what will woman be?

. . . not yet fully seen

. . . not yet fully revealed

. . . but coming

. . . coming

. . . what will woman be?

In search of Her
LIFE

Woman, seeking a sense of who she is, of how she wishes to live her daily life, letting its patterns and rhythms express her deepest values . . . Woman, today, under a pressure, faced with the temptation to live out her life in the realm of the masculine, denying her own needs, mistrusting her fatigue, ignoring the anguish of her own struggle.

Her task will be to gain the help and support of her inner masculine side and to return to the values of the Archetypal Feminine as she grounds her life in an order and clarity that nurture her.

Grounding her being

. . . and the daughter Persephone searched for her mother Demeter even while the mother yearned for and searched for her daughter,

. . . the Great Mother reaching out Her arms to Her daughters . . . the energy of the Eternal Mother flowing out to each woman in her individual life, stirring, strengthening her own unique feminine spirit.

Woman of this day yearned for by the Mother, warmed by the presence of the ancient Maternal, reaching back to be nurtured by it, to nurture it in return.

. . . sensing a presence affirming her care of body, affirming her sexuality and her respect for its sacredness, reawakening her to the rhythms of her own life, the cycles of nature . . .

. . . an ancient energy embracing woman of this day, making her newly aware of her needs for quiet, centeredness, presence . . . an ancient sense of being, asking woman to trust it again, to embrace it, to ground herself in it . . . through her own individual sense of life, to ground herself in the beingness of the Eternal Feminine.

Woman grounds herself in being as she nurtures the elemental, caring for her own matter through rest and through touch.

Woman grounds herself in being as she nourishes herself with food and furnishings so harmonious with the earth that her own nature is made more harmonious, rather than set at odds by a conglomeration of celluloid, styrofoam, and fabrication.

Woman grounds herself in being as she fulfills the simple daily tasks, the care of household and workspace, with a devotion of the heart, as she quietly arranges her books, washes a tiled floor, or polishes a lamp, polishing her own sense of life alongside it.

Woman grounds herself in being as she claims her time, moment by moment, to *be* within it, as if she could touch it and hold it in her hand . . . as she claims her time to *be,* not forcing into an hour more than that hour can hold, but listening, with a sense of balance and restraint, that each task be quietly fulfilled with pause before and after . . . an interlude for her to reflect, to be present to herself.

Woman grounds herself in being as she claims a settling . . . settling into time and space, She may resist moving her household each third year, as corporation, military, or ministry dictate, so that she may remain long enough in one place to grow familiar with the sounds and spaces of her home, the corners, nooks, and crannies offering refuge to body and spirit alike . . . the humming of the furnace . . . the creaking of the cellar stair . . . the whispers of the summer evening as the shadows of the bamboo blow across the window.

Her center, her substance finally acknowledged,
woman can keep alight the candle of her being,
her deep and quiet wisdom of life,
now reflecting outward in ever-widening
circles of serenity and stillness
her microcosmic inner mystery
mirrored and
mirrored again
in the macrocosm surrounding her.

A woman in her seventh decade of life had a dream:

*"I dreamed of a silver key, which seemed very plain at
first, but becomes more beautiful as my life goes on.*

*I reach into the inside of a very old tree. The tree is
rotting away . . . soft, beautiful, rich russet brown. I
know just where to reach but not what I will find. I
pull out an old key fastened to a newer one. One is a
common silver house key such as you could buy in any
store . . . the other, gold, very old, ornate, is from an
Arthurian legend.*

*There is no sense that I know what to do with it, why
the two keys are fastened together, For fastened, fused
as they were, they could not be used. Someone comes
and grabs for my key . . . but I grasp it firmly."*

"I worked with the dream image a long while. I hoped to be able to separate the keys someday so that they could be used . . . the gold Arthurian key, made of the precious metal of the masculine, from the silver one. Later it was always the silver key made from the precious metal of the feminine that appeared in my dreams.

"That key, that plain, ordinary, silver key, is unlocking my life to me and showing me how to live it . . . I am having to give up a wish for making things 'special' all the time. Now, for me, the special times are the most ordinary . . . long days when I have a sense of the day stretching out quietly before me with enough time to put into it what it will hold, and without any special wonderfulnesses.

"Time to <u>be</u> . . . in the garden, in the house . . .
    ordinary time . . .
        time to just be and to breathe . . .
            time . . . unlocked to me, to live."

How might your life have been different, if, as a young woman, there had been a place for you, a place where you could go to be with women? A place where you could be received as you strove to order your moments and your days.

A place where you could learn a quiet centeredness . . . to help you ground yourself in daily patterns that would nurture you through their gentle rhythms . . . a place where, in the stillness at the ending of a task, you could feel an ancient presence flowing out to sustain you . . . and you learned how to receive and to sustain it in return.

How might your life be different?

Gathering her wholeness

Late afternoon . . . late autumn . . . five women gather to write of their lives. Each seeking to touch a ground within herself, a solidity, a place to rest. Each, like many in today's world, seeking a substance within where she may be at home.

For them, as for many women, the struggle to recognize that inner substance is made more difficult by the criticizing voices in the culture and in their own animus, not yet fully differentiated. These voices may negate, for each woman, the very thing that is the stuff of her own substance—her woundedness, her softness, her quiet strength, even her beauty or grace. Again and again, a woman must deal with the inner criticism of her animus. In its raw form, it presses its collective masculine value system upon her, acknowledging only its own heady logos qualities as worthwhile, and seeking to poison her against her own needs to embrace the qualities of the Eternal Feminine within herself and to bring them forth in her life.

Especially in those women who have earlier developed the logos functions in their professional endeavors, who may have lived out a part of their lives in energetic and dominant animus-effectiveness, the wish will make itself strongly felt to embrace, to return, to come home, full circle, to a feminine ground.

And if ever the fear or nagging guilt comes that she has meaninglessly isolated herself or become quiescent, she need only remember from the study of alchemy that, even while the individual works diligently and waits prayerfully for inner transformation and wholeness, her work is reflected in a transformation in the greater realm: the wholeness manifesting in the life of one individual becomes a microcosm of wholeness effecting an alchemical change in the macrocosm of the outer realm . . . wholeness begetting wholeness.

> Woman, with a candle lighted
> to help her keep faith with her own life . . .
> a centered presence
> spreading in concentric circles around her.

❖ ❖ ❖

Late afternoon, the slanting rays of late autumn sun touch the five women. The first writes:

> *"The days are getting shorter, the nights longer . . . The cold is coming. it is time to listen to the darkness now, to acknowledge it . . . to take in its wisdom.*
>
> *"I've been more in touch with my own anxiety and sadness. I've allowed myself not to hide it under a pile of achieving busy-ness. I'm allowing myself to cry when I feel sad . . . and then I feel better . . . more balanced, whole . . . That's part of me, too.*
>
> *"When my daughter wept, last week, with all her sorrows, I was able to be there for her, not frantic, not needing to find an answer, but simply there, able to stroke her lovingly and be a witness to her pain . . . the pain we all have in one way or another but that, thank God, is only a part of the human condition."*

Gathering her wholeness

❖ ❖ ❖

The second, a tall beautiful woman, an economist, fifty-five years old, was about to re-enter professional life, and afraid of losing what she had found in the years since she had last been employed. She wrote:

> *"How good to come to be with women and feel I can be myself, I am myself. As soon as I sat down, I felt sadness . . . let myself feel it . . . sad, and somewhere behind it, tearfulness . . . all that's been missing in my relationship to myself and to others . . . I've been too up, outgoing, joking, optimistic . . . holding up a false persona.*

> *"Sadness is part of emotional wholeness for me . . . I am more human when I feel it . . . it softens me. I have needed it."*

The third woman, newly embracing her life after a threatening illness, wrote:

> *"There is a sense that is growing in me . . . on my daily walks that are my movement meditation . . . I'm beginning to fill up the hole inside, to people my inner space.*

> *"I'm looking at broken places in my life and seeing how real they are . . . they <u>are</u>, my pain <u>is</u>, I <u>exist</u> . . .*

> *"They are there and real, and I am not hollow, but whole."*

❖ ❖ ❖

The fourth woman, nearing her sixtieth birthday, a woman who had risen high in her profession, wrote:

"I am so aware, at my age, of light and dark. Earlier in my life, I was all light, swift, clever, bright. I dressed in primary colours and abhorred anything that I considered slow, dull, muted.

"It was only when I lived through the summer solstice light, far above the Arctic Circle, the light of the longest day in our year, the totality of white, white, ever-pervasive light, day after day, that I experienced our desperate need for darkness, for shadow, for relief from the clarity, sharpness, and rationality that this present world demands . . . a need for soft lines, blendedness, greys . . . to respect one's need to be sometimes out of focus, unformed, blurred.

"Now, the winter returns, the darkness . . . the year, come full circle again . . . a chance, again, to sink into one's own stillness . . . a time to feel one's fatigue, the aches of life, one's own age, to reconnect, once again, with a deep, dark, earth-energy, hidden far below in our roots.

"The winter is for us to nurture ourselves in that same way—a long time of preparatory darkness and inchoateness . . . a very long time to nurture and to begin to begin to bring forth . . . A time when it is in the natural order of things to be still, to rest in the quiet blackness. A time to trust that one will be refreshed and brought again to new creativity just as is all the rest of nature . . . to trust, once again, in the cycles of light and darkness in nature herself and within one's own nature."

Gathering her wholeness

❖ ❖ ❖

The fifth woman, gifted with abundant dramatic and musical ability, never certain of whether she possessed it, or it her, wrote:

> "For me, the balance between doing and just being is the most important and dangerous question. If I am guilted or lured into achieving too much and lose the stillness at my center, then it takes me a long time to regain it, and I do violence to myself or those I love because of fatigue and pressure.

> "I have had to give up 'winning big' because I love my life when I am connected to it, and I hate it when it and I get caught up in competition and deadlines. Then I have an overriding sense of impatience . . . my foot taps . . . I swallow food whole, I spill the coffee as I pour it, I burn myself on the stove . . . I rip, and wrench, and tear. There is a violence that takes over every act and shrieks orders at me.

> "I am finding that it takes a lot of time to be a woman, to have a feeling of space and breath, a chance to sink into myself . . . as long as I take time every morning to light a candle to my life, it remains my life. But if I hurry into work without that small moment of quiet, then I've already lost myself, and the day. The task, for me, is to care, daily, for myself and my life . . . to love and to nurture, within myself, moment by moment, the quality of quiet presence, quietly being present to my life, which sanctifies it . . . to live as if the candle is lighted."

How might your life have been different, if, through the years, there had been a place where you could go? . . . a place of women, away from the ordinary busy-ness of life . . . a place of women who knew the cycles of life, the ebb and flow of nature, who knew of times of work and times of quiet . . . who understood your tiredness and need for rest.

A place of women who could help you to accept your fatigue and trust your limitations, and to know, in the dark of winter, that your energy would return, as surely as the spring.

Women who could help you learn to light a candle and to wait . . .

How might your life be different?

Embracing her woundedness

Once, in a group of women, gathered monthly to spend a day together, stood a hag.

She was short and ugly, fashioned from a length of log, stood on end, given a frayed hemp rope for hair, acorns and seeds for face, torn burlap for a cloak, and finished, in her loathsomeness, with a tail.

She was recognized at once by the women as the embodiment of shame, horror, fear—of all which is anguished, not allowed, and cast out. She carried the pain that hurts too intensely to be borne. Instead, we deny it and rise above it, to remain, smilingly, "all right" in our own eyes. We seek a life of distraction or service to others, choosing to see the anguish in them, rather than in ourselves.

And the paradox, even if those we serve truly need help, is that if we are not open to our own anguish, to the orphaned child within, we harden ourselves and become busy, cheery dispensers of aid. We become unable to truly nurture or be present to either woundedness or healing.

For only by being present to the woundedness within ourselves can we be present to the woundedness in others. Their woundedness and anguish must be related to and embraced. It must be experienced in all its pathos. The woundedness of each of us must be fully owned and fully suffered for it to receive succor and be comforted.

It was late in the day. Each woman had named her issue, speaking quietly into the silence . . . how she viewed her life, her place in it, her responsibility to herself. The small creature stood at the center of the circle, a quality of being about her that would not be denied. Shamed and judged or not, she was present to herself.

As the shadows cast by the winter sun lengthened and the room fell into darkness, a woman picked up the small urhag and rocked it in her arms.

In the hush that followed, several women wept. It was what was to be, simple and natural—as if a howl, a cry shrieking from inner and outer darkness, had been heard. The wild, banshee terror of pain and torment that we all desperately wish not to own had finally been embraced. At last, here was a place for it to be cradled, comforted. At last, a place for it to come home, to rest.

The women asked, "How can we help ourselves and each other to own our terror, our own shame, our own abandonment? How can we give it a place to come home to, so that it may cease its endless wandering?

"How can we listen for a still, small voice that says, 'The orphaned child within each of us is howling in terror, No more. No more violence. Let us be here in our pain and sorrow. Let us be here, present, to our anguish. Let us acknowledge it, cradle it, and comfort it.'

"Let us give it a place to come home, to rest."

Embracing her woundedness

The creature in us needs comfort, nurture and holding, and deprived of the soft, holding, maternal, withers and dies. Years ago in well-known laboratory experiments, baby monkeys languished when fed mechanically from a twisted, cold wire figure but prospered when comforted by a softly pillowed form. We seem predisposed to forget this most basic lesson.

Only woman can gestate a return to a deeper feminine consciousness containing that holding. By acknowledging her center and her needs, she can allow an ancient awareness, uniquely feminine, to re-emerge . . . an awareness with substance and strength as well as softness.

Only out of woman, conscious of her feminine grounding and the world's desperate need of it, can be born a new awareness, strong enough to contain the anguish and anxiety of civilization driving itself to the breaking-point, fragmenting under its burden of terrorism and torture.

It is as if the whole world were a latchkey child waiting wistfully and fearfully at the door, hoping to be let in to the warmth and nurture it so deeply needs to sustain it . . . waiting to hear a voice, a new clear feminine voice of substance, softness, and strength, "Come home . . . to rest."

How might your life have been different, if, one day, during your monthly stay in the Women's Lodge, you had suddenly felt fearful? If, even in those safe surroundings, you felt the dread and panic you sometimes felt in your life away from there? And, what if, as you tried to express your anguish, a woman had listened to you . . . another woman, somewhat older, had listened quietly, intently, as you expressed your fears, your experiencing of your own shame and abandonment?

If there had been a stillness, a grave silence in that moment, as your eyes looked into the eyes of the woman who listened, and you saw that she was there, present to your suffering . . . that she was there, so present to your terror and woundedness that she helped you, also, to embrace your own anguish . . . and give it a place to rest . . .

How might your life be different?

Finding her voice

An old woman, her shoulders wrapped in a grey woolen shawl, spoke softly:

"I ask, What is asked of us? And the answer comes . . . To come, each one of us, to our own voice . . . our own feminine voice. It is an enigma that when a woman first expresses herself, even if it is a matter for which she cares deeply, it may emerge in a false-masculine voice. It may state her matter factually, but without the shadings and overtones from her own life . . . without the nuance of her womanly feeling values. Or, if she is ill at ease, she may hand her script over to the animus and let him play the role for her, not out of her feelings, her relatedness and vulnerability, but out of an abstracted, polished, harder side of herself that feels a pressure to have all the answers, that has lost touch with softness, uncertainty, and weakness.

"What is asked of us? To find a voice . . . a voice to cry out . . . to make us all attend to our woundedness, our pain, our anguish, our needs . . . in ourselves, our children, our men . . . in nature, itself . . . that vast woundedness which has been so ignored, so denied . . . to attend that woundedness, and, at last, to honour it . . . the woundedness of us all . . . in hope and faith that it may heal."

The old woman smoothed the shawl around her neck.

"What is asked of us at this time? Our lives, as women, have vastly changed. We may finally rise in the professions, politics. Now the irony is that as men reexamine an old exaggerated emphasis on success, women feel more and more pressure to be successful, even to be extremely successful. It is as if the young woman of today were being asked to make up for the inequities of the past and to sacrifice her own

life as she does it. She is urged to place her children in corporate day care facilities and to feed herself and her family from prepackaged supermarket stock. Her inner and outer children, any young, tender parts needing special understanding and care, must go unmothered. As she is urged to put her energies in service to dehumanizing systems, her own individual life and her needs for domestic privacy disappear.

"Surely there must be another way! A way not yet fully revealed, in which we women may reconnect with our ancient feminine grounding and come to a new and more conscious realization of it . . . a way of new stature and new position in the world, while still maintaining the values of the private, the inner, the contained and subjective.

"I want to reach out my hand to touch the arm of the woman of today and support her in not letting the animus pull her into collective expectations of success and pull her life away from her, moment by moment . . . Support her in not letting the glare and dazzle of what is publicized wash away her grounding in her own life. I want to tell her to keep faith with herself through her walks, her reflecting, her quiet care of her life.

"I want to comfort her and say, 'Ah, young woman, hold on to your voice, your subjective stance, the voice of your individual life. Do not let it be taken from you. It is the very soul of humanity and needs to be cherished and heard. As you claim your place in the world, your authority, perhaps even a position of political power, stay true to your grounding in the ancient feminine. Do not rise above your own creaturely needs, but make the quiet nurturing of them the center of your life.' "

A late afternoon chill filled the air. The old woman brushed a strand of grey hair from her face.

"I ask myself what is asked of us . . . And the answer comes: Our whole lifetime is asked . . . to encompass our own birthing. First, we must hold ourselves within, in privacy and darkness, protecting what is there, while it is young and fragile, from being revealed too soon, when it could be undone by premature criticism. Then, when our time is come, we must act as our own midwife and be present to our own process as it comes to birth.

"We women must listen to ourselves and to each other as the individual voice of each of us is born. We must learn to discern, to stay in proper relationship to the animus . . . to simply listen and be present to one another. If another woman is wonderfully original, then the animus will make us envious and make us want to criticize or denigrate her. When I remember how my own old counselor, a wise, patient woman, simply listened and drew me out, it helps me not identify with the envy, but listen quietly as a younger woman searches for her own voice.

"Most helpful of all for a woman to remember as she seeks her own voice, is that it will emerge only when she speaks from her own true nature and experience, only when she expresses what she cares most dearly about and is her own unique and individual truth. If she makes the mistake of identifying with the Archetypal Feminine and becomes intoxicated with its powerful energy, if she takes up its cause, she is likely to be devoured by it. Her task must be to ground herself in her own life and let its truth emerge."

The old woman shifted, resting her weight against the door frame.

"I see a finely wrought chain of tempered silver, delicate, yet strong, stretching back through time, reaching deep into the earth . . . A chain of women, each listening to each, being present to her as she waits for herself to be born, for her feeling values to come to form and to birth . . . Woman after woman after woman, being present, as each finds her voice."

The first snowflakes of the season drifted slowly towards the earth. The old woman pulled the shawl more snugly around her shoulders.

"I ask what is asked of us, and I know that the answers and attitudes for a new feminine consciousness will not be found in the collective realm. They will not come from the mass, but from the voice of each individual woman as she seeks, tentatively and hesitantly, to live out her life in the values of the ancient feminine.

"Perhaps what is asked is that each of us come to her own renewed grounding in the Archetypal Feminine, come to a conscious awareness of that grounding . . . a conscious awareness, understanding, and embracing of it in her own being and her own life."

How might your life have been different if there had been a place for you, a place of women? A place where other women, somewhat older, had reached out to help you as you rooted yourself in the earth of the ancient feminine . . . A place where there was a deep understanding of the ways of woman to nurture you in every season of your life. A place of women to help you measure your own stature . . . to help you prepare and know when you were ready.

A place where, after the fires were lighted, and the drumming, and the silence, you would claim, finally, in your Naming, as you spoke slowly into that silence, that the time had come, full circle, for you, also, to reach out . . . reach out as younger women entered into that place . . . reach out to help them prepare as they struck root in that same timeless earth.

How might your life be different?

Woman, standing on a hillside, peering,

peering into blue space . . .

. . . what will woman be?

. . . not yet fully seen

. . . not yet fully revealed

. . . but coming

. . . coming

. . . what will woman be?

The Author

Judith Duerk

Born in the Midwest of a family with strong religious ties, Judith Duerk followed the call of her early love for music. She earned B.S. and M.S. degrees from The Juilliard School, studied as a postgraduate at the Mozarteum in Salzburg and at Indiana University, and taught music at the university level before beginning preparatory work in the fields of psychotherapy and music therapy.

For many years, she has led groups of women on Retreat. She says, *"I am awed by the depth of healing that comes as women sit in a circle, by the power of women keeping silence together, and by the truth in their sharing."* In addition to her daily work as therapist, she teaches T'ai Chi Ch'uan and works with the ancient Taoist healing art of Chi Kung.

Judith notes that the sensitivity and spiritual strength of the men around her have been helpful role models for her animus. Her two sons are grown. She recalls that *"when they were younger, they liked to joke that all their mother cared about was Yin-Yang-Jung . . . but they really knew better."*

Her husband is a woodsman and artisan. Their lives together have been deeply nurtured by the greater cycles of nature, and they seek to know how to nurture those cycles in return.

Deepening your Circle

Ideas to help draw your circle of women together:

Over the last ten years, in hundreds of women's circles around the country, women have gathered to study Judith Duerk's books. In a typical evening, one woman may read a single chapter aloud while the others sit listening, with their eyes closed. And then at the end, they may share their personal experiences or images—or perhaps memories from old dreams—that are evoked during the reading.

Your circle may want to reflect on the ending questions for each chapter, *"How might your life have been different if . . . ?"* You may want to expand your reflection with the discussion questions offered here.

You may want to begin your circle the way Judith often begins her retreats: She asks the women to imagine that they are inviting the important women from their lives to join them, to sit just slightly behind them in the circle, all of the women from their whole life . . . those who were supportive and affirming, and perhaps those who might have been, but weren't . . . "the special woman teacher who reached out to you in second grade, the favorite auntie who always made you the lemon crisp cookies, the kindly neighbor lady who plucked the red tulip and gave it to you over the fence . . . and the woman professor or mentor who taught you so much." Consider your relationship with each of these women, positive and negative. Let them all be there surrounding you in your gathering of women.

Reading Group Suggestions
for *CIRCLE OF STONES*

IN SEARCH OF HER MOTHER

The universal importance of woman's tears
(pages 29-32)

This chapter describes a dream in which a woman is criticized for her tears. Have you felt criticized or demeaned when you cried? What is your sense of our culture's acceptance of tears? What were *you* taught about crying: Were tears seen as a sign of strength or a sign of weakness? What is your experience of the value of tears?

How it was before . . . (pages 33-38)

Page 38 describes a possible celebration of a first menstrual day. What happened on *your* first menstrual day? How might it have been different for you if this day had been joyously celebrated? How might you want to celebrate with your own daughter(s) or niece(s)?

"Yes, sadness . . ." (pages 39-44)

Women once had a strong connection to the mysteries of life, to the primal elements of nature, to the Great Mother. How might *your* life be different if you carried an inner image of a Great Mother as a source of comfort, substance, and strength? How do you think women today would benefit from a renewed connection with the Great Mother?

Then, saying goodbye . . . (pages 45-47)

This chapter is about a woman leaving behind her role in an organization. There is a statement on page 46 that "somewhere deep inside, she knows that she must leave to become herself." What might you need to think about leaving behind in your life to become yourself? An excess of meetings and time commitments? An overwhelming sense of duty? A life of service that leaves no room for yourself? What kind of support can you imagine receiving from other women that would help you trust and nurture your journey of becoming more fully yourself?

IN SEARCH OF HER SELF

A sense of her depth (pages 55-58)

This chapter is about our deepening to grow more fully into ourselves. "A woman, searching for herself, must descend to her own depths . . . As she descends, a woman touches a strength, a certainty that changes her" (page 56). What is your experience of this? How might it have been different for you if other women had been there to help you "go inside yourself"?

A sense of her feelings (pages 59-64)

This chapter describes a woman who had been taught to be dutiful, moral, and productive. What have you been taught about being "dutiful" and "productive"? How does this affect your ability to feel your own feelings? Were you ever encouraged to express your own feelings? How might it have been different for you if you had been encouraged to express your feelings rather than contain them?

A sense of her process (pages 65-69)

"Depression comes as a gift asking that a woman recognize her own substance and trust it as the quiet, steady voice of her own truth" (page 66). In what ways can you imagine depression being a gift? How have your own times of depression connected you more deeply to your own truth?

A sense of her fear (pages 70-74)

Page 72 suggests that a woman can be helped by hearing another woman's experience of suffering/depression. Has another woman ever shared with you about her own depression? How might your life have been different if there had been a woman who had been willing to be with you during periods of pain and anger and sorrow?

A sense of her need (pages 75-79)

As the woman in this chapter tells her story of an over-extended lifestyle, she observes, "The way we women treat ourselves is shocking . . . we expect ourselves always to be Amazons, with all the emphasis on achieving, on appearing 'all right.' " (page 76). In what ways do you identify with this? Have you ever experienced an illness or depression that caused you to stop trying to prove yourself and start taking care of yourself? What did you learn from this experience?

A sense of her self (pages 80-85)

This chapter describe the process and necessity of a woman breaking out of the collective societal mold in order to reclaim her life as her own. How has our society encouraged or discouraged this? How have the people in your own life encouraged or discouraged you from breaking out of the mold? In what ways have you changed the "script" prescribed for you? What were the results?

IN SEARCH OF HER LIFE

Grounding her being (pages 93-97)

This chapter depicts a number of ways in which woman grounds herself: with food and furnishings, in the simplicity of daily tasks, in claiming her own time and place. How do *you* ground yourself? Where do you go or what do you do to feel centered?

Gathering her wholeness (pages 98-103)

This chapter portrays five women gathering to explore their inner lives. What difference do you think women might make in today's fast-paced living and chronic busyness if women set aside time for this kind of deep sharing? What difference would it make in your own life? How could you begin?

Embracing her woundedness (pages 104-107)

This chapter poses that, unless women can be present to their own woundedness, they cannot be truly present to the woundedness in others. Yet, our culture seems impatient with woundedness. What is your experience of this? Have you ever been present to someone else's woundedness? Has anyone ever encouraged you to pay attention to your own woundedness? How has it been helpful?

Finding her voice (pages 108-112)

"Hold onto your voice, the voice of your individual life. Do not let it be taken from you. It is the very soul of humanity and needs to be cherished and heard" (page 109). What does this means to you? How do you get in touch with your own individual voice?

❖ ❖ ❖

At the end of each section of this book, there is a two-page poem in which the question is posed, "What will woman be?" What is your vision for the impact women will have on our culture during the next ten years? What is your vision for how *your* life will be different in the next ten years because of the support of women?

Let the circle continue . . .

I Sit Listening to the Wind
Woman's Encounter Within Herself
JUDITH DUERK

Gentle yet provocative reflections that call women to rebalance the Masculine/Yang energy—which spiritual traditions have called "the Wind"—with the ancient values of the Feminine/Yin.

"Extraordinarily valuable. [Judith] gently draws you into a moonlit circle of women to share their moments of longing, tears, and joy, and discover within yourself the silent center of your being. The rhythm of her writing reverberates long after you reluctantly close this book."—Karen Signell, Ph.D., C.G. Jung Institute of San Francisco; Author of *Wisdom of the Heart*

"A nourishing, tenderly understanding, helpful book."—Jean Shinoda Bolen, M.D., Author of *Goddesses in Everywoman* and *Crossing to Avalon*

1-880913-37-2 Quality Paperback $13.95

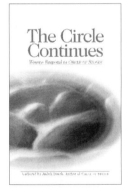

The Circle Continues
Women Respond to CIRCLE OF STONES
GATHERED BY JUDITH DUERK

In celebration of the 10th anniversary of Judith Duerk's beloved *Circle of Stones*, Innisfree Press issued a worldwide "call for writing and art," inviting women to share their stories, poems, and art in response to the question, *"How has the affirming, sustaining presence of women made a difference in your life?"* The selections chosen for *The Circle Continues*—representing sixty women from eight countries—are a chorus of art, reflection, and poetry, celebrating the strength, compassion, and wisdom of women.

1-880913-50-X Quality Paperback $15.95